Dad Jokes
Are Just How
Eye-Roll!

Jimmy Brewer

Copyright © 2018 Jimmy Brewer

All Rights Reserved

This book may not be reproduced in whole or in part, by any means now known or yet to be invented, without the express written permission of the Copyright Owner, excepting brief quotes used in reviews or scholarly journals. The purchase of a copy of this book does not confer upon the purchaser license to use this work or any part therein in other works, including derivatives.

Why should you respect the pickle?
It's kind of a big dill!

There's a fine line between the numerator and denominator!

What did the horse say after it tripped?
"Help! I've fallen and I can't giddyup!"

Two swans walk into a bar, the third one ducks.

Did you hear about the circus fire?
It was in tents!

Don't trust atoms.
They make up everything!

What do you call a cow with two legs?
Lean beef.

What do you get when you cross an elephant with a rhino?
Elephino!

I only know 25 letters of the alphabet.
I don't know why!

What do prisoners use to call each other?
Cell phones.

How do you make an octopus laugh?
With ten-tickles!

Why did the man name his dogs Rolex and Timex?
Because they were watchdogs!

What's the difference between a poorly dressed man on a tricycle and a well-dressed man on a bicycle?
Attire!

Can February March?
No but April, May!

I was addicted to the Hokey Pokey, **but I turned myself around**!

Why was the man scared of German sausages?
He feared the wurst!

What's the best way to watch
a fly fishing tournament?
Livestream!

Did you hear that Arnold
Schwarzenegger will be
starring in a movie about
classical music?
He'll be Bach!

The rotation of earth really
makes my day!

Are you all right?
No, I'm half left.

I had a dream that I was a muffler last night.
I woke up exhausted!

Son: Dad, how do I look?
Dad: With your eyes!

What is Beethoven's favorite fruit?
A ba—na-na-na!

Did you hear about the man who was hit in the head with a can of coke?
He's all right, it was a soft drink.

Why did the melons have a wedding?
Because they cantaloupe!

Son: Dad, do you enjoy making courthouse puns?
Dad: Guilty!

Hostess: "Do you have any reservations?"
Dad: "No. I'm confident I want to eat here!"

I'm reading a book about anti-gravity.
It's impossible to put down!

You're American when you go into the bathroom, and you're American when you come out, but what you are while you're in there?
European!

Did you know the first French fries weren't actually cooked in France?
They were cooked in Greece!

If you see a robbery at an Apple Store does that make you an iWitness?

Spring is here! I got so excited I wet my plants!

A sandwich walks into a bar and orders a Coke. The bartender says, "Sorry we don't serve food here."

I bought some shoes from a drug dealer. I don't know what he laced them with, but I was tripping all day!

What do you call a factory that sells OK products?
A satisfactory!

I used to have a job at a calendar factory but I got fired because I took a couple of days off.

Why do scuba divers fall backwards into the water?
Because if they fell forward they'd still be in the boat!

Have you ever heard of a music group called Cellophane?
They mostly wrap!

What kind of magic do cows
believe in?
MOODOO!

What time did the man go to
the dentist?
Tooth hurt-y!

Son: Dad, I think broken my
arm in several places.
Dad: Well don't go to those
places!

Why did the dad give the
pony a glass of water?
**Because he was a little
horse!**

Atheism is a non-prophet organization!

Ho do you know when you've slept like a log?
You wake up in the fireplace.

What cheese can never be yours?
Nacho cheese!

A police officer caught two kids playing with a firework and a car battery. He charged one and let the other one off.

Did you hear about the kidnapping at school?
It's fine, he woke up!

I went to the zoo the other day, and there was only one dog in it.
It was a shitzu!

What did the daddy tomato say to the baby tomato?
Catch up!

What do you call a cow with no legs?
Ground beef!

So a duck walks into a
pharmacy and says,
**"Give me some chap-stick
and put it on my bill"**

Why did the scarecrow win an
award?
**Because he was
outstanding in his field.**

Why did the boy smear
peanut butter on the road?
To go with the traffic jam.

Why does a chicken coop
only have two doors?
**Because if it had four
doors it would be a
chicken sedan.**

Why won't seagulls fly over
the bay?
**Because then they'd be
bay-gulls!**

Two peanuts were walking
down the street.
One was assaulted.

Where does batman go to the bathroom?
The batroom!

What's the difference between an African elephant and an Indian elephant?
About 5000 miles!

What do you call Jay—Z when he's sleeping?
Jay Zzzzzzzzz.

What's the advantage of living in Switzerland?
Well, the flag is a big plus!

A red ship and a blue ship have just collided in the Caribbean.
Now the survivors are marooned.

I've deleted the phone numbers of all the Germans I know from my mobile phone.
Now it's Hans free.

How much does a hipster weigh?
An Instagram!

What do you call a group of
killer whales playing
instruments?
An orca-stra!

Why was the big cat
disqualified from the race?
Because it was a cheetah!

Bicycles can't stand on their
own, they're two tired.

I just watched a documentary
about beavers.
***It was the best damn
program I've ever seen.***

How do you make holy water?
You boil the hell out of it!

Do you know where you can get chicken broth in bulk?
The stock market!

What did the ocean say to the shore?
Nothing, it just waved!

Why do crabs never donate to charity?
Because they're shellfish!

What do you call an
Argentinian with a rubber
toe?
Roberto!

What do you call a man with
no nose and no body?
Nobody nose!

I cut my finger chopping
cheese.
*I think I may have grater
problems.*

What do you call a fish with
no eyes?
A fshhhh!

What do you call a man with
no arms and no legs lying in
front of your door?
Matt!

How do you know when your
cat is sick?
It stops feline well.

I dreamt I was drowning in
an ocean made of orange
soda last night.
But it was just a Fanta sea.

A termite walks into a bar
and asks, **"Is the bar
tender here?"**

Why do you never see
elephants hiding in trees?
**Because they're so good
at it!**

What happened when the two
antennas got married?
**The ceremony was kind of
boring, but the reception
was great!**

What did one snowman say
to the other one?
Do you smell carrots?

How do you make a tissue
dance?
**You put a little boogie in
it!**

Dad: Why are you staring at
the orange juice container?
Son: It says concentrate!

I wanted to buy some
camouflage pants the other
day, but I couldn't find any.

How do you organize an
outer space party?
You planet!

What do you call a belt with a watch on it?
A waist of time.

What kind of shoes does a thief wear?
Sneakers!

A jumper cable walks into a bar. The bartender says, "I'll serve you, but don't start anything."

I went to a seafood dance last week and pulled a mussel.

Did you hear about the man
who stole a calendar?
He got 12 months!

How many apples grow on a
tree?
All of them!

How does a penguin build its
house?
Igloos it together!

How can you tell if an ant is a
boy or a girl?
**They're all girls, otherwise
they'd be uncles!**

What is Forrest Gump's
password?
1forrest1!

Did I tell you the time I fell in
love during a backflip?
I was heels over head!

Son: Dad, did you get a
haircut?
Dad: No, I got them all cut!

I would avoid the sushi if I
was you.
It's a little fishy.

What's brown and sticky?
A stick!

Want to hear a joke about paper?
Never mind it's tearable!

Did you hear about the restaurant on the moon?
Great food, no atmosphere!

Why did the cookie cry?
Because his father was a wafer so long!

What did the mountain climber name his son?
Cliff!

Did you hear about the dad who invented Altoids?
They say he made a mint!

www.ingramcontent.com/pod-product-compliance
Lightning Source LLC
Chambersburg PA
CBHW070105260726
48658CB00002B/986